# BILL WALTON

## MAVERICK CAGER

**Library of Congress Cataloging in Publication Data**

Hahn, James
    Bill Walton: maverick cager.

    (Their Champions and challengers 1)
    SUMMARY: A biography of the controversial captain of
the Portland Trail Blazers who has strong opinions about
athletes' public and private lives.
    1. Walton, Bill, 1952-    —Juvenile literature. 2. Basket-
ball players—United States—Biography—Juvenile litera-
ture. [1. Walton, Bill, 1952-    2. Basketball players] I.
Hahn, Lynn, joint author. II Title. III. Series.
GV884.W3H33 796.32-3'0924 [B] [92] 78-9447
ISBN 0-88436-443-7

Published 1978. Produced by EMC Corporation
180 East Sixth Street, Saint Paul, Minnesota 55101
Printed in the United States of America
0 9 8 7 6 5 4 3 2 1

# BILL WALTON
## MAVERICK CAGER

BY JAMES & LYNN HAHN

EMC CORPORATION ST. PAUL, MINNESOTA

The temperature zoomed up to 85°F. in Portland, Oregon on June 5, 1977. A deep blue sky topped the city. The air smelled fresh and clean. It was a beautiful day to be outside. Yet, many people either stayed home and watched television or kept their ears close to radios.

Why? Because they were infected with a disease known as Blazermania! What's Blazermania? It's how you feel if you're a Portland Trail Blazer fan and your basketball team has only to win one more game to be World Champions.

That Sunday afternoon, thousands of excited fans packed themselves into Portland's Memorial Coliseum. Later, even police radios squawked the score to patrolling squads every few minutes. No one wanted to miss a second of this basketball game.

The best-of-seven National Basketball Association (NBA) championship series did not begin well for the Portland Trail Blazers. The Philadelphia 76'ers won the first two games. Many basketball fans and sports reporters said the Sixers would easily win the championship.

But not Bill Walton, Portland's captain and brilliant center. Bill has a mind of his own. He was convinced the Trail Blazers could still take it all.

Bill's acrobatic rebounds, frightening blocked shots, zinging passes, slam dunks, smooth lay-ups, classic hook shots, his cheers and yells—his brilliant leadership on both offense and defense—turned the series around. He led the Trail Blazers to three straight victories over the 76'ers. Before game six began, the series stood three games to two, with the Trail Blazers one game ahead.

Game six started fast and furious. Before the 76'ers knew what was happening, Bill Walton zipped a pass back to Bob Gross near the basket—a perfect back door play! Two points! Then, seconds later, another crowd-pleasing back door play from Walton to Gross. Two more points!

The Sixers looked like they didn't know where to stand, who to guard, where to dribble, or when to shoot. If the Sixers double-teamed Walton, he'd pass to an open teammate. If they didn't guard Bill closely, he'd shoot and score.

Bill's hustling defense upset the 76'er offense. On one play, Philadelphia's Julius Erving, also known as Doctor "J," leaped towards the hoop for what seemed like an easy lay-up. But suddenly, from several feet away, Bill Walton jumped up. With the body control of a ballet dancer, he blocked the shot. Not used to such treatment, Doctor "J" could only shake his head in amazement.

Portland led most of the game, but Philadelphia refused to give up. With 18 seconds left in the game, the Trail Blazers' lead was only two points, 109-107. With Doctor "J" operating, the Sixers were still alive!

Bill's both a defensive and offensive player.

The clock wound down and Philadelphia had the ball. Suddenly, Floyd Lee had a chance to tie the game. He shot. The ball arched towards the basket. Timing his leap perfectly, Walton jumped up and slapped the ball away. The referee signaled a clean block. No goal tending! But Sixer George McGinnis, only twelve feet away from the basket, grabbed the loose ball. Desperately jumping up, he shot. The ball sailed towards the nets. When it hit the rim, it bounced away from the bucket. Walton tapped the rebound to his teammate, Johnny Davis.

Suddenly, the buzzer blared! The game was over! Portland had won the right to be called the best basketball team in the world! Bill Walton was so happy he yanked off his sweat-soaked jersey and threw it to the crowd of joyous Blazer fans. Blazermania broke out everywhere!

Sports reporters voted Bill Walton the series' most valuable player, mostly because of his leadership. Bill's 20 points, 23 rebounds, seven assists, and eight blocked shots in the last game sealed his election. But, more importantly, Bill Walton reached one of the goals he'd been aiming at for a long time—capturing the NBA championship for Portland.

Bill's climb to the top of the professional basketball world was not easy, physically or emotionally. The Bill Walton story begins on November 5, 1952 when Theodore and Gloria Walton become the proud parents of a son, William Theodore Walton.

Bill Walton does not like to take credit for Blazermania—he is a team player.

The Walton family lived in La Mesa, California, a middle-class suburb near San Diego. It's about 125 miles south of Los Angeles. Clean, neat, and white, Bill's home nestled into a southern California hillside.

Bill's parents did not push him into sports. In fact, they wanted him to spend much of his free time practicing the baritone horn. When Bill was about seven years old, he began playing basketball almost everyday. Bill says he had a lot of fun going out in the backyard and shooting baskets.

To widen his experiences, Bill's parents encouraged him to play team sports. As a nine-year-old, Bill began playing organized baseball, football, and basketball at Blessed Sacrament Elementary School. In the fourth grade Bill learned how to play team basketball from Frank Graziano, a volunteer coach at the school. The coach drilled Bill and his teammates in basic basketball—passing, dribbling, free throws, lay-ups.

At Blessed Sacrament, Bill played guard on offense because he was such a good dribbler, passer, and playmaker. Because he was such a good rebounder and could block shots, Bill played center on defense.

With his red hair and freckles, many people said Bill looked like Huckleberry Finn. But he didn't have Huck's prickly personality. In grade school, Bill was quiet, thoughtful and shy. When he was excited or nervous, he sometimes stuttered.

Bill's climb to the top began when he was a high school student.

As Bill matured, his mother and father taught him to love all people and help those who were in need. Bill's father could have earned more money from a job with a private business. But he chose to help people as a caseworker with San Diego's Public Welfare Department.

A librarian, Bill's mother made sure there were plenty of books around the house. When he wasn't playing basketball, Bill did a lot of reading. To help him in school, Bill's parents advised him to read every day and develop good study habits. Bill's parents had lots to do with the beliefs he has today and his strength in standing by them.

In the fall of 1966, Bill became a freshman at Helix High School in La Mesa. He was about six feet tall then, but was skinny and looked weak. When he played sports, he often tired easily.

While playing on the freshman basketball team, Bill tore some cartilage in his left knee. The injury required surgery. Bill spent many weeks hobbling around school on crutches. To strengthen his knee again, Bill had to do tiring leg exercises. He recovered in time for the next basketball season.

But while he was a sophomore, Bill still felt weak after playing several minutes in a basketball game. He worked hard at practice, but had trouble keeping up a steady, strong pace. Because of his lack of strength, Bill played on the junior varsity basketball team. He couldn't keep up with the varsity pace.

Even though Bill wasn't playing for the varsity team, he had a good attitude. He cheered for the team to win and worked at building up his own strength.

In the fall of 1968, Bill started his junior year in high school. He stood 6' 7'' and weighed about 185 pounds. That year he made the varsity basketball team. He had quick moves around the basket, was an accurate passer, and could score many points.

But towards the end of practices and games, Bill still felt weak and tired easily. Bill says his legs would begin to feel heavy in the third and fourth quarters. Bill worked hard to build up his strength. He began to improve with every game.

Bill had a good attitude in high school. His beliefs got him in trouble when he attended UCLA.

Bill worked so hard and improved so much that by the end of the season he was leading the varsity in rebounds and points. His outstanding play helped Helix High win the California Interscholastic Federation district tournament title. After the season, Bill was voted to the national All-Star Prep Team.

As Bill became older and older, he grew taller and taller. One of the reasons was heredity. Both his parents are tall. His dad is 6′ 4″ and his mom is 5′ 10″. Another reason—Bill liked to eat. Some days Bill would down several hot dogs for breakfast! Other days, hamburgers would be his breakfast food. Bill says his mom's great cooking was the main reason he grew so tall. For supper, she'd cook delicious steaks and roasts. And Bill would eat and eat and eat.

In the fall of 1969, Bill's senior year, he stood 6′ 10½″ and weighed about 196 pounds. He was stronger then and could finish most basketball games without feeling so tired and winded.

With his long, thin fingers extended high over the rim, Bill snared many offensive and defensive rebounds for Helix High. His quick, straight out-let passes sparked many fast breaks for his teammates. That season, Bill made more than half the baskets he attempted.

Opposing teams tried to stop Bill by double teaming him. That hardly ever worked, so they triple teamed him. That didn't stop Bill either. He still rebounded, passed and scored again and again. Some teams used zone defenses to try to stop Helix High. But Bill and his teammates just passed around, over and through the zones to score and win.

Bill helped Helix High to a 33-0 record that season. He scored 958 points, averaging 29 points per game. His shooting rate figured out to an amazing 70%. In other words, for every ten times Bill shot, seven sliced the nets for scores. And in every game Bill pulled down about 22 rebounds. Those statistics helped Bill land a spot on the high school All-American team.

Bill's private, closed-mouth attitude upset and surprised the press while he was in high school and in college.

Because Bill was such an excellent high school basketball player, many sports reporters wanted to tell their readers all about this extraordinary young man. But Bill was—and still is—a private person. He doesn't want to be famous. He feels uncomfortable when sports reporters ask personal questions about his life off the basketball court.

Bill says his play on the basketball court is enough news. His personal life should be kept private. Some reporters, Bill says, don't respect his privacy. For example, one day when he was in high school, Bill read his name and the name of a girl he was dating in a large city newspaper. The reporter wrote a story about where Bill and his date went and what they did. Bill says that story was an invasion of his privacy. He never wanted anything like that to happen again. It made him very angry.

After Bill finished playing basketball for Helix High, many colleges throughout the country asked him to enroll at their schools. They wanted him, not only because he was an excellent basketball player, but also because he was an excellent student. He ranked 29th in a class of 575. Bill's father stopped counting the scholarship offers after they passed 100.

Bill wanted to go to a school that offered excellent educational programs as well as excellent sports programs. Learning was just as important as playing basketball. Bill says, "Good teachers are just as important as good coaches."

After carefully examining all the scholarship offers, Bill finally decided to enroll at the University of California at Los Angeles (UCLA). He felt they offered him the best educational and athletic programs.

In 1970, the year Bill became a UCLA freshman, the National Collegiate Athletic Association (NCAA) still had rules keeping freshmen from playing varsity sports. So Bill spent the season playing on UCLA's freshman basketball team.

John Wooden, UCLA's legendary varsity basketball coach, wanted Bill to strengthen his arms and legs. College basketball was much harder to play than high school basketball. To build up his strength, Bill would have to do a lot of running.

One reason Coach Wooden's basketball teams won so many games was they hardly ever made mistakes. Instead, they caused other teams to make mistakes. So, as a freshman, Bill practiced and practiced—basic dribbling, passing, rebounding, and shooting.

Coach Wooden says, "Bill Walton was eager to learn UCLA's basketball style. He was very coachable." He adds "At times, Bill was puzzling, impatient and inconsistent. But most of the time, he was friendly, open and sincere." Even though they had some disagreements, especially over the length of Bill's hair, Coach Wooden says he liked Bill Walton, he liked him a lot. Bill just flatly refused to be anything but himself.

Bill's great height and jumping ability often kept him out of "goal-tending" range.

Bill helped lead UCLA's freshman team to a 20-0 season. His 362 points, 320 rebounds, and his rate of making baskets, 155 out of 226 attempts—68.5%, earned him the Seymour Armond trophy as UCLA's most valuable freshman basketball player.

Still, the shy, soft-spoken young man guarded his personal life and privacy. He didn't talk to sports reporters because he felt what he did before and after basketball games was nobody's business but his own. That was it.

UCLA's famous coach, John Wooden, found Bill to be sincere but puzzling
at times.

Bill had to keep his knees bandaged. He played in constant pain.

In the fall of 1971, as a college sophomore, Bill began playing varsity basketball for the UCLA Bruins. After only a few games, many fans, coaches and sports reporters said he was the greatest college player in the history of the game.

Somehow, Bill overcame the pain and kept playing.

They said Bill Walton was better than Bill Russell and Lew Alcindor (now known as Kareem Abdul-Jabbar) had been in college.

Why? Because Bill Walton was an all-around basketball player. He could play offense and defense easily and skillfully. Bill shot, passed, rebounded, and blocked shots without making many mistakes.

Coaches said Bill Walton was the ideal team player. He'd rather pass than shoot and would only shoot when he couldn't find a teammate open. Sports reporters said Bill was a brilliant basketball player. He directed both the offense and defense. And fans said Bill was exciting and mysterious.

**Bill did not start on the varsity team.**

**Young fans are amazed at Bill's skill.**

During 1971-72 Bill helped UCLA to an undefeated season and a spot in the NCAA championship game against Florida State. In that game, Bill scored 24 points, snared 20 rebounds, and blocked four shots. UCLA won 81-76. Bill was voted the most valuable player of the tournament.

Throughout that season, Bill still would not talk to sports reporters. He didn't want the publicity. He said he was a team player. The others players should be interviewed. They all worked as a team. Reporters were puzzled and put off. They did not understand Bill. And they didn't like his closed-mouth attitude.

For Bill, his sophomore statistics did all the necessary talking—633 total points, 21.1 points per game; 238 of 372 field goal attempts for a 63.9% shooting rate; 157 of 223 free throws for 70.4%; 466 rebounds for 15.5 per game.

Those statistics become all the more amazing when you know that Bill played with constant pain. He suffered from tendonitis, a redness and swelling of the tendons around the joints. Tendonitis can be caused by rapid growth of the legs, such as Bill had in high school.

Before every game, Bill had to put heated pads on his knees. This loosened the ligaments and tendons so he would not feel so much pain during the game. Immediately after every game, Bill had to hold ice packs on his knees for thirty minutes to keep the swelling down. Bill fought his pain privately. Fans and reporters would not know about it until years later.

**Bill feels that his performance on the courts speaks for him.**

When Bill wasn't playing basketball, he studied hard, majoring in history. Bill also took courses in African-American affairs because he wanted to learn about black people and prevent prejudice. Bill earned good grades, about a B+ average and was named to the Academic All-America team. But Bill says he studied hard "to learn, not to get good grades."

Because Bill Walton did and still does care about all people—black, brown, red, white, and yellow—he decided to join the people who were against the United States fighting in Vietnam. Bill said the United States was involved in an immoral and illegal war. He said he wanted the United States military to stop killing people and get out of Vietnam so the Vietnamese could decide what they wanted by themselves.

**Bill's appearance changed. His ideas and actions upset many people.**

One day, Bill and several other UCLA students decided to protest the war by sitting down in the middle of Wilshire Boulevard, a large Los Angeles street. Because this was breaking the law, Bill was arrested and fined $50. The sports reporters went into an uproar. Athletes weren't supposed to be politicians. They hounded Bill more than ever. Bill only tried to stay out of their way. Again, he guarded his privacy.

He spent the summer of 1972 taking several long bicycle trips, backpacking into wilderness areas, and reading. Two of his favorite authors are John Steinbeck and Kurt Vonnegut, Jr.

In the fall of 1972, Bill began his junior year at UCLA. He stood 6' 11" and weighed 225 pounds. John Wooden's coaching, Bill Walton's passing, rebounding, blocking, and shooting and the skillful play of the entire UCLA team led UCLA through another undefeated season to the NCAA tournament.

Many sports reporters, coaches, and fans say Bill Walton's play in the 1973 NCAA championship game against Memphis State was the greatest exhibition of basketball skills in the history of college basketball. In that game, Bill made 21 of 22 shots! He scored 44 points; snared 13 rebounds; blocked 7 shots! UCLA won 87-66, claiming its seventh straight national title and 75th straight victory.

**Bill agrees to sign autographs but always gives credit to other members of his team.**

Still, Bill did not brag or boast about his play. Instead, he shyly walked into the Memphis State locker room and told the players they played great and shouldn't feel bad because it was only a game.

During the 1972-73 season, Bill scored 612 points and grabbed 506 rebounds. For the second straight year, Bill Walton was named the best college basketball player in the United States.

During Bill's last season at UCLA he and the basketball team experienced something strange —they lost some basketball games. Notre Dame, Oregon and Oregon State defeated them. In the NCAA tournament, after two overtimes, UCLA lost to North Carolina State, 80-77. Bill didn't feel angry or upset that UCLA lost the NCAA title. He congratulated North Carolina's players, saying they played a great game.

In February of 1974, Bill received the James E. Sullivan Memorial Award as the most outstanding amateur athlete in the United States. The only other college basketball player ever to receive this award was Bill Bradley of Princeton, over ten years earlier.

During his senior year, Bill thought about playing professional basketball. He'd received several million-dollar offers to quit school and play in the pros. But he turned them down because he didn't want to leave his coach, his teammates or his studies.

After the basketball season, Bill decided he'd like to test his skills with professional basketball players. He said money wasn't that important to him. He really wanted to play for the challenge and enjoyment that professional basketball offered.

The Portland Trail Blazers drafted Bill and he agreed to play. During the summer of 1974, Bill said he wanted to get his mind ready for playing professional basketball. He spent many hours reading, meditating, backpacking, and bicycling in Oregon. Bill says he enjoyed the peace and solitude of the mountains, streams, and trees. On a large wooded area, near the Willamette River, Bill had a A-frame house built. He spent many happy hours there alone.

In the fall of 1974, Bill began practicing with the Portland Trail Blazers for the 1974-75 professional basketball season. He worked hard. The fans, reporters, and coaches all looked forward to an exciting, winning season with Bill Walton leading the team.

After playing some games, Bill suddenly said he could not play any more. He said his ankle hurt him too much. Doctors examined the ankle and found a bone spur, a painful calcium deposit on the bone. Some sports reporters said Bill Walton really didn't want to play pro ball. They claimed many basketball players had bone spurs, yet played with pain.

Bill said his ankle hurt him every time he played. This time, the pain was too much. He didn't want to risk more injuries, and he wouldn't play until his ankle was better. He had suffered enough in college.

Because Bill believes drugs are harmful to his body, he refused to take them for the pain in his ankle. Bill didn't play in many games. Fans who had bought season tickets were very disappointed.

**Bill's first season with the Trailblazers was disappointing.**

**Bill, often with ice on his knees between plays, as above, to ease the pain.**

Bill played in a few games when his ankle didn't hurt. But then he caught the flu. Many people said he got sick because he didn't eat a proper diet. In college Bill stopped eating flesh foods, such as meat and fish. He didn't want to eat slaughtered animals, and said meat was harmful to his body. Bill also stopped eating other foods he considered unnatural, such as candy and soda pop. Bill believes you are what you eat. He says if you put garbage in your body, you will be garbage. His diet is mainly vegetables, fruits, nuts, and grains.

Because of the flu, Bill lost a lot of weight. He became too weak to play professional basketball. Many people said if Bill started eating meat again, he would get stronger. Bill's diet remained the same. He stuck by his beliefs.

Bill did not play for several weeks. When he finally played in a few games, he looked weak, tired easily and played poorly.

Then rumors started spreading that Bill didn't like Portland's weather. Some reporters claimed Bill said he wasn't getting enough sun in Oregon. Bill believes the sun gives his body energy. There were even some reports that Bill wanted to be traded to Los Angeles. Portland said Bill had a contract and couldn't be traded.

Several more weeks passed before Bill played again. Then he said his ankle was hurting. He refused to play. Many people said Bill was letting Portland down. His first season in the pros was certainly not as good as his college years. Playing in only 47 of 82 games, Bill only averaged 12.8 points, 12.6 rebounds, and three blocked shots per game. People wondered what had happened to Bill Walton. His pro statistics were about half his college statistics.

After his rookie season, Bill set out to prove he could play professsional basketball. In the summer of 1975, he worked hard to build up his strength and get in shape.

To build up his weight, he ate huge meals of vegetables, fruits, grains and nuts. He often ate several pounds of potatoes for breakfast. But he didn't eat any meat. He lifted weights for six hours every week, played volleyball, and did a lot of bicycling.

When Bill wasn't training, he enjoyed watching the sun rise over the mountains at his cabin. He listened to tapes of Bob Dylan, the Grateful Dead, and Country Joe and the Fish. Bill says "these musicians help me see life clearly." Bill was sure that he was ready to tackle professional basketball.

But Bill's second season in the pros was also disappointing. Because of personal and physical problems, Bill played in only 51 games. Some of his personal problems received national publicity. One of Bill's best friends is Jack Scott, a political and sports reformer. During the basketball season, rumors spread that Jack had hidden Patty Hearst, who had been kidnapped and was later involved in a bank robbery. While checking the rumors, the Federal Bureau of Investigation (FBI) investigated Bill Walton because of his friendship with Jack Scott.

Finally Bill agreed to talk to reporters. Interviewed on national television, Bill Walton said the FBI had "tapped" his telephone, was harassing him, and was the "enemy."

Bill's remarks upset many people. Again, they said Bill should play basketball and stay out of politics.

Bill said people shouldn't try to limit his freedom, try to figure him out, or try to define him. He said he was more than a basketball player. He was a total person, with a right to his own beliefs.

Bill Walton sincerely believes there is more to life than sports. He says "People make sports more important than they really are. Most sporting events are blown up out of proportion."

Bill says life isn't a fairy tale. There are problems that people can help solve. When he isn't playing basketball, Bill says he wants to help needy people.

Proving that he really is more than a basketball player, Bill has helped organize fund-raising events for the American Indian Movement (AIM) and some environmental projects. Bill's also had some thoughts about becoming a lawyer, giving free legal help to people who can't pay for lawyers. Being a farmer, teacher, or forest fire fighter also interests him. Bill says money can't buy him happiness. He knows many rich people who aren't happy. But helping people always makes him happy.

At the start of the 1976-77 basketball season, Bill said he was healthy. For the first time he didn't have to think about pain before, during, and after every game. Bill had a new attitude. He was anxious to play. After watching his leadership and dedicated play, Bill's teammates elected him their captain. Bill's play that season led Portland to victory after victory. He had stuck-out the disappointing seasons. He had taken on the challenge of professional ball.

After watching Bill's skills on the court that season, many fans, sports reporters, and coaches said he was the best all-around center in the history of professional basketball. They said Bill Walton combined the best of Bill Russell's defensive play, the best of Wilt Chamberlain's powerful play, and the best of Kareem Abdul-Jabbar's offensive play in his own brilliant basketball style.

The way Bill plays proves he really is a brilliant basketball player. He may be the most intelligent team leader ever to play the game.

On defense, he knows how to get into the right place at the right time, grabbing almost every rebound in sight. Bill's back door passes on offense shatter many defenses. Playing unselfishly, he passes off instead of "gunning" every time his hands touch the ball. He is not a "big ego" player.

Bill played in all but 17 games in 1976-77, averaging about 20 points per game. He led the NBA with about 15 rebounds per game. Many people said Bill was playing in more games and playing better because he finally matured. He had cut his hair and trimmed his beard. Bill said his record improved because he was feeling better. He didn't have to feel pain every second. He said he cut his hair because long hair didn't feel good any more. But, he said, "I still say and do what I believe."

Bill changed his hairstyle and his diet.

Believing that flesh foods really are not good for his body, Bill still refuses to eat meat. He doesn't even drink tap water. He sips distilled water or fruit juices instead. A typical breakfast for Bill is a quart of orange juice, a vegetable omelet, and rice. Raw vegetable salads, whole grain breads, pasta, fruit juice, and fruits are on Bill's lunch and supper menus.

After playing basketball for almost twenty years, Bill says he still enjoys the game. He loves to play defense—rebounding and blocking shots. On offense, he enjoys zinging perfect passes to start fast breaks.

Bill says he likes to play in pressure games because they make him play better basketball. He still practices hard, working on the basics over and over. He likes to play without making any mistakes. After leading the Portland Trail Blazers to the NBA championship, Bill said he would keep on trying to do better.

Bill says he enjoys basketball so much that if he wasn't playing organized basketball, he'd be playing in pick-up games in school yards and gyms.

Becoming a brilliant basketball player was not easy for Bill Walton. He had to conquer both physical and personal problems.

Then, something unusual happened. Even for a maverick like Bill, it was unusual. Just 14 months before, Bill had led Portland to an NBA title. Suddenly he mysteriously wanted to be traded. Why? Finally someone leaked word to the press—Bill had injured his foot. The Trail Blazers' doctor had given Bill a shot for the pain. Bill kept playing. Now, 16 weeks later, his foot had not healed. Some doctors said it was broken. They said it had been broken a long time. The Trail Blazers should have known that, some claimed.

The saddest rumor was that the brilliant center might never heal correctly. He might never be able to play professional ball again.

Bill had never given too much of his private life to the public but he had given all that he could on the basketball court. Now it seemed that maybe Bill had given too much on the court after all. Only time will tell for Bill Walton, maverick cager.

Bill Walton, a brilliant maverick in professional sports.

# BASKETBALL GLOSSARY

*assist:* pass of ball that helps directly to score basket

*back door play:* pattern of play that helps make basket

*block:* to stop the movement of another player

*blocked shot:* an attempt to shoot the ball that's stopped

*bucket:* the basketball net

*center:* player in central position on team

*defense:* actions or players that keep other team from scoring

*double-team:* two players guarding one player on other team (triple-team-three players guarding one)

*dunk:* to drop the ball into the net, sometimes forcefully (slam dunk)

*fast break:* team moves as quickly as possible to make a basket, once they get the ball

*free throw:* player tries to throw from the free throw line to make one point

*goal tending:* unallowed play when player touches the ball at net and keeps other team from scoring

*guard:* stays with player of other team to prevent scoring

*hook shot:* player standing with his/her back to basket, looking over his/her shoulder, throws ball at basket in an arc

*lay-up:* throw made when player reaches by jumping as close to net as possible to shoot ball

*offense:* actions or players that are intended to make score

*open teammate:* team member not closely guarded

*pass:* to throw the ball to another player

*playmaker:* player who directs teammates on court

*rebound:* getting control of the ball after a missed shot

*shoot:* throwing the ball and trying to make a basket

*zone defense:* each player guards a certain area in front of basket they are defending